HEALTHY TREES, HEALTHY PLANET

Anne Flounders

RED
CHAIR
•PRESS•

Please visit our website at **www.redchairpress.com**.
Find a free catalog of all our high-quality products for young readers.

Healthy Trees, Healthy Planet

Publisher's Cataloging-In-Publication Data
(Prepared by The Donohue Group, Inc.)

Flounders, Anne.

Healthy trees, healthy planet / Anne Flounders.
p. : ill., maps ; cm. -- (Our green Earth)
Summary: The quiet nature of trees hides the fact that trees are always working for us. Their biggest, most important job is playing a role in making Earth and our environment healthy. Learn some of the ways trees help, why they are in danger, and what you can do to help protect them. Includes step-by-step ideas for taking action, different points of view, an up-close look at relevant careers, and more.
Includes bibliographical references and index.
ISBN: 978-1-939656-44-5 (lib. binding/hardcover)
ISBN: 978-1-939656-32-2 (pbk.)
ISBN: 978-1-939656-51-3 (eBook)
1. Trees--Juvenile literature. 2. Forest ecology--Juvenile literature. 3. Environmental protection--Juvenile literature. 4. Trees. 5. Forest ecology. 6. Environmental protection. I. Title.
QK475.8 .F56 2014

582.16   2013937163

Illustration credit: p. 8-9: Joe LeMonnier

Photo credits: Cover, title page, p. 4, 5, 6, 10, 11, 12, 13, 14, 15, 16, 17, 18, 19, 20, 21, 22, 23, 26, 27, 31, back cover: Shutterstock; p. 25: Collin Buntrock; p. 28, 29: Andrew Berry; p. 32: © Hildi Todrin, Crane Song Photography

This series first published by:
Red Chair Press LLC   PO Box 333   South Egremont, MA 01258-0333

Printed in the United States of America

1 2 3 4 5 18 17 16 15 14

MIX
Paper from responsible sources
FSC
www.fsc.org   FSC® C002589

# TABLE OF CONTENTS

CHAPTER ONE

Trees Help the Environment

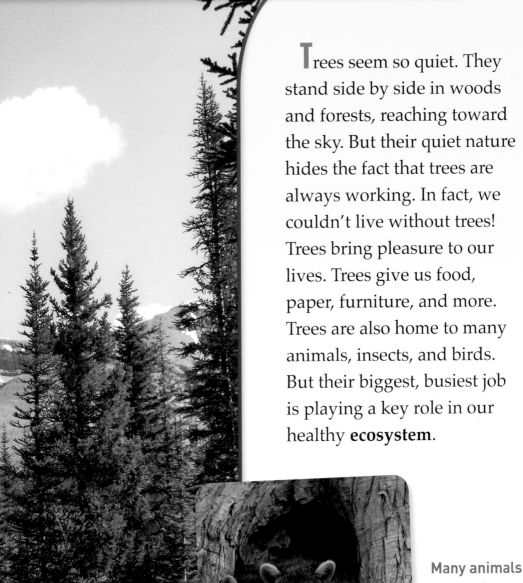

Trees seem so quiet. They stand side by side in woods and forests, reaching toward the sky. But their quiet nature hides the fact that trees are always working. In fact, we couldn't live without trees! Trees bring pleasure to our lives. Trees give us food, paper, furniture, and more. Trees are also home to many animals, insects, and birds. But their biggest, busiest job is playing a key role in our healthy **ecosystem**.

Many animals make a home in trees.

Trees clean the air so that we may all breathe easily and stay healthy. Whether it's a palm tree in Hawaii, a larch tree in Russia, or an ash tree in Spain, all trees work the same way. Trees absorb **carbon dioxide** from the air. They also filter out air pollutants. In return, trees then put clean oxygen into the air. Oxygen is the gas we need to breathe.

One tree can take 10 pounds of pollutants out of the air each year. It can make enough oxygen for two people to breathe for a year.[1]

Trees are good for Earth in other ways, too. They help to keep our waterways clean. Trees act as a natural filter for water that travels from the ground into lakes, rivers, and seas. Trees absorb excess water after a storm.

[1] Source: American Forests

DID YOU KNOW?
There are more than 23,000 species of trees in the world.

Tree-roots hold soil in place and keep it from washing away. That process of soil breaking down and washing away is called erosion. If too much soil washes away from an area, nothing can grow there.

Trees are a key part of the water cycle. They take moisture from the soil and put it into the air. Later, it comes back down as rain.

The Water Cycle

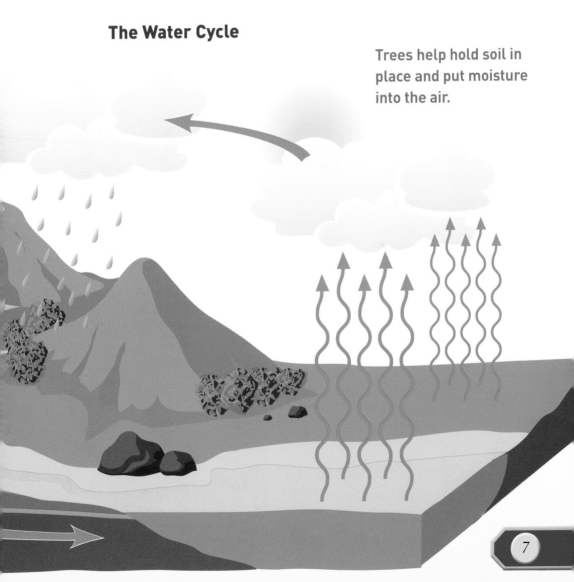

Trees help hold soil in place and put moisture into the air.

Where in the World Are Trees?

Trees grow almost everywhere on Earth. Forests are large, dense groups of trees that cover a great deal of land. Forests cover about one-third of the Earth's land area.

There are three types of forests.

Tropical forests are found on or near Earth's equator. They are hot and wet. Tropical forests cover only about 7 percent of the Earth's land, but they are home to about half of the world's plant and animal species!

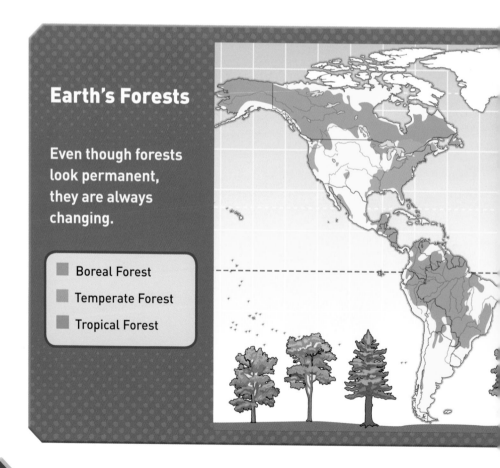

Earth's Forests

Even though forests look permanent, they are always changing.

- Boreal Forest
- Temperate Forest
- Tropical Forest

Temperate forests are found in North America, Europe, and Asia. They have four seasons. Oak, hickory, beech, hemlock, maple, and willow trees are just some of the trees one might find in a temperate forest.[2]

Boreal forests are the largest forests. They stretch across the northern lands of Canada, Alaska, Russia, and Europe. Evergreens such as pine, spruce, and fir trees grow in boreal forests. These forests are sometimes called *taigas*.

The map below shows the location of the world's forests.

[2] Source: NASA Earth Observatory

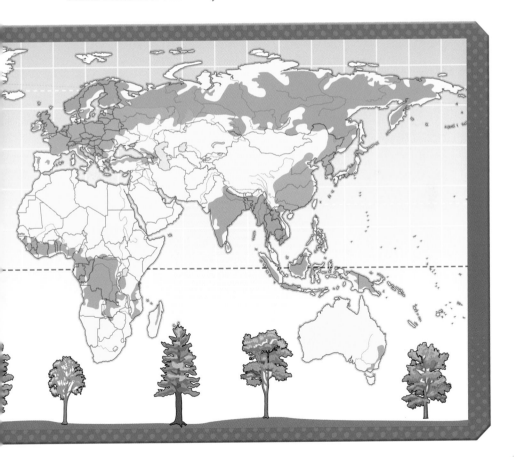

What Comes from Trees?

Trees give us many things we would have a hard time living without. People use all parts of a tree. The trunk of a tree gives us lumber. We use lumber to build homes, furniture, and other wood items. Leftover wood chips and sawdust are used to make pulp for paper. The **bark** of a tree gives us products such as cork, oils, and dyes. **Cellulose** is a group of tiny fibers that hold wood together. It is used to make paper, fabrics, carpet, thickeners for food and cleansers, cellophane, and cosmetics. Tree **sap** is used in products such as maple syrup, sweeteners, chewing gum, ink, soap, cleaners, cosmetics, and glue. We eat a variety of fruits, nuts, and spices from trees.

We eat: fruit, nuts, chocolate, maple syrup, gum

We use: wood, rubber, cork

We make: paper, cardboard, insulation, furniture, cabinets, houses, medicine, fuel, paint, turpentine, rayon, melamine, linoleum, cleaning products

Trees give us things we use for our basic needs of food, clothing and shelter.

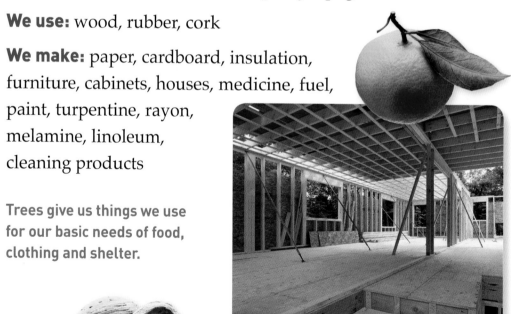

At Home in a Tree

While people live in homes made from trees, many animals make their homes in trees. A tree can be a **habitat** for insects, birds, reptiles, amphibians, and mammals.

Tree frogs live in trees. They have special pads on their toes that help them cling to a tree and move around it without falling onto the ground.

The barred owl is just one type of owl that lives in trees. This owl needs to live in a moist forest. Owls glide through a forest looking for food on the ground.

tree frog

barred owl

koala

orangutan

Koalas only eat the leaves of the eucalyptus tree. These trees are found in Australia. Koalas spend their whole lives in eucalyptus trees. They come down to the ground only to move to another tree.

The name orangutan means "old man of the forest." Young or old, male or female, orangutans all live in trees. Their hands, feet, and long arms help them swing, climb, hang, and grip—important skills for tree living!

CHAPTER TWO

Problems Trees Face

Trees do much good for Earth, but there are many threats to trees and their habitats. One major problem is **deforestation**. That is the removal of forests from the land. People have been clearing forests from the land for thousands of years.

Forests in Brazil and Thailand are lost to farming.

Why are forests removed? It may be to make way for a large-scale farm or ranch. It may be to build roads, neighborhoods, or businesses. Deforestation may occur when many trees are needed for lumber or fuel. The forests we lose each year equal the size of Greece.[3] About half of the forests that once covered the Earth are gone.

A soy field in Brazil was cut into this tropical rainforest.

One area of worry is the Amazon River region of South America. Millions of acres of tropical rainforests have been cut down. Many have given way to cattle ranches and soybean farms. There is high demand for those products.

Remember, trees clean the air by taking carbon dioxide out of it. The carbon dioxide is stored in trees and their roots. When large areas are cleared, the gas stored in trees is released into the air. That contributes to global warming.

[3] Source: The GreenFacts Initiative

Amazon River

These trees were lost to a wildfire.

Deforestation does not always happen on purpose. Other causes of forest loss are **drought** and wildfires. A drought is a long period of time in which there is much less rainfall than is normal for an area. Trees die or become weak. Weaker trees are more likely to develop diseases.

Wildfires are on the rise, too. Why? Warm seasons have grown longer. That is when wildfires happen. Forests are drier. Fire spreads easily among dry trees. There is more lightning with storms. Lightning sparks fires. Uncontrolled wildfires put too much carbon dioxide into the air. That contributes to climate change, which leads to more wildfires.

Disappearing American Forests

For thousands of years, forests thrived in North America. Before the arrival of European settlers, about half of what is now the continental United States was covered in forests. Today about 90 percent of those forests have been removed. Of the forests that remain, most are on land protected by the government.

In some cases, new forests are growing. But it can take up to 100 years for a new forest to grow. The new forests may be very different from the original ones.

THE AMERICAN CHESTNUT

The American chestnut tree once stood in forests stretching from Maine to Mississippi. People harvested chestnuts. They used its wood to make good, strong furniture. The fast-growing trees thrived, often reaching over 100 feet tall. But in 1904, chestnut trees began to develop a **blight**, or illness. The blight had been brought to the United States from Asia on imported plants. They could not be saved. Within 40 years, the once mighty American chestnut tree was gone. About 3.5 billion trees were lost to the blight.

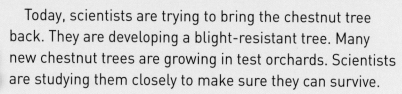

Today, scientists are trying to bring the chestnut tree back. They are developing a blight-resistant tree. Many new chestnut trees are growing in test orchards. Scientists are studying them closely to make sure they can survive.

Trees can be **endangered**. Right now, about 8,000 species of trees worldwide are at risk of being lost.

The whitebark pine is one threatened tree **species**. It is found in western United States. It plays an important role in helping to reduce erosion and flooding caused by melted snow. The pine's seeds are an important food source for many birds and animals. Its loss could cause many problems throughout the western ecosystem.

But loss of the tree's habitat, disease, wildfires, and the environmental effects of climate change have taken their toll on the species. In two or three generations, the whitebark pine may be gone.

Whitebark pines can be found in Oregon's Crater Lake National Park.

The U.S. Forest Service is taking steps to save the species. Many of the trees are on U.S. Forest Service land. One way the agency is helping is by developing and planting new whitebark pine seedlings that can resist disease.

CHAPTER THREE

People Help Trees

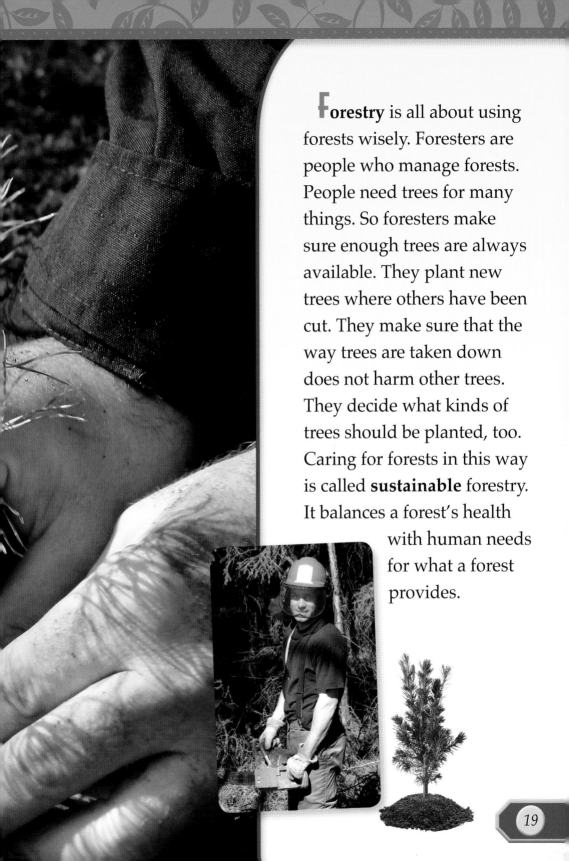

Forestry is all about using forests wisely. Foresters are people who manage forests. People need trees for many things. So foresters make sure enough trees are always available. They plant new trees where others have been cut. They make sure that the way trees are taken down does not harm other trees. They decide what kinds of trees should be planted, too. Caring for forests in this way is called **sustainable** forestry. It balances a forest's health with human needs for what a forest provides.

Many people are working hard to protect Earth's trees. One way people help is by planting new trees. Sometimes these trees replace other trees or whole forests. In 2003, California's largest known wildfire burned most of the 25,000-acre Cuyamaca Rancho State Park near San Diego. After a wildfire, a forest can often restore itself. Seeds from the old trees can grow from the ashes. But in Cuyamaca, the fire was so hot that it destroyed the seeds as well as the trees. The forest could not recover on its own. Many groups worked together to replant and regrow the forest. Today, trees and other plants are growing there again.

Four Threats to Trees

Deforestation	Climate Change	Development	Pollution

Much of North America and Europe lost forests centuries ago. Loss of forests now is greatest in parts of Brazil, Indonesia, and central Africa.	As Earth becomes warmer, there are more wildfires and stronger storms. Climate change also means more pests and disease to harm trees.	By 2030, nearly 22 million more acres of U.S. farm and forested land will be developed. That's about the same size as the entire state of Indiana.	Trees soak up and store carbon dioxide. It helps them grow. But too much CO_2 and ozone from pollution may lead to slower growth and decay.

Central Park, New York City

Urban and Community Foresting

In cities, a big threat to trees is development. The more homes and buildings that are built in a city, the more trees are cut down. But trees are just as important in cities as they are in forests. They keep the air clean. They help manage storm water, which can prevent flooding and other damage. They help control temperature, which can save energy. Studies show that tree-filled urban areas are safer and healthier than those with only a few trees.

Many cities and towns across the United States are making trees a priority. They know the value of having trees. If trees are removed in an area, they try to replace them with new trees. The new trees may be in the same spot or nearby.

Developers' Dilemma

Sometimes new homes or businesses are planned for land that is covered in trees. In some cases, the developer is able to keep some of the trees. But in other cases, trees are removed to make way for new construction. Between 1982 and 2001,

about 10 million acres of forest were cleared for building. That number continues to rise.

In 2012, a home-builder in Georgia planned to build new houses on a ten-acre piece of land. The land had been woods, thick with trees. Neighbors in the area were surprised and saddened when the builder cut down every tree. He explained that he needed to make way for 19 new houses. It was a neighborhood where people were eager to live.

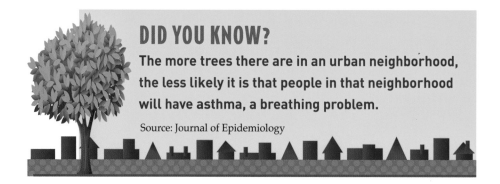

DID YOU KNOW?

The more trees there are in an urban neighborhood, the less likely it is that people in that neighborhood will have asthma, a breathing problem.

Source: Journal of Epidemiology

FACE OFF: Land to Build

A developer buys land and makes plans to build on it. But sometimes that land is covered in trees. What happens then?

"Can't the owners of the land do whatever they want with it? That's their right. The new neighborhood might be in a great location where people want to live. To make money, a developer needs space to build lots of homes or new stores. New trees can be planted later."

Cities and towns have rules about how trees are handled when there is new development. Many towns want to preserve trees. Rules vary from city to city. They might have a builder keep a certain number of trees. Or they may say new trees must be planted if many are cut down. The city may also have a say in which trees are cut down and which are kept.

"It's sad that so many healthy trees are taken away just to build more houses or to build a mall. If they have to build on the woodlands, I think they should keep some of the old trees. Those tall trees will make the new neighborhood look much better."

There are good reasons to keep healthy trees in their place. Trees do add value to a neighborhood. They look attractive. People buying a newly built home might pay more if the land around the home has mature trees. And, of course, trees help the environment. In some cases, neighbors may petition, or ask, a city to require a builder to keep certain trees.

What do you think?

Everyone Can Help Trees

People can help trees through their everyday choices. Here are a few ways greener choices can protect trees.

Save energy. By using only what you need, fewer fossil fuels are burned for energy. That means less carbon dioxide goes into Earth's atmosphere. Less carbon dioxide means fewer problems related to climate change. And that's good for trees.

Recycle paper and cardboard. The paper you recycle goes to make new things. You can look for and buy recycled paper products. That means fewer trees need to be cut down for paper and other goods.

Encourage your city's planners to plant more trees. More trees mean cleaner air, cleaner water, and more shade to control temperature. More trees mean prettier spaces and happier people and animals.

Eat beef and lamb from North American ranches. Rainforests in South America are being cleared for ranches. If there was less demand for food from these ranches, there would be fewer trees cut. Eating less meat overall helps even more.

Reduce your need for paper products. Buy products with less packaging, such as bulk-sized boxes of cereal. Think twice before printing something out. Use both sides of a piece of paper. Cancel catalogs that you don't read. Read the newspaper online. Use cloth napkins. Reuse gift bags or wrap gifts in reusable cloth, rather than using wrapping paper.

COLLEGE TO CAREER

Do you think you might be interested in a career that helps trees thrive for the future?

Here are just a few of the jobs you could do.

Habitat Manager *Smokejumper*
Park Ranger *Timber Specialist*
Research Ecologist *Urban Parks Planner*

COLLIN BUNTROCK

Collin Buntrock grew up in a small town surrounded by cornfields. But as a forest management student at the University of Wisconsin, Collin enjoys working with farmers and landowners on how to take care of the forests on their land. "About 60 percent of my time is spent connecting with people about their land. Forestry is about trees, but it's also about wildlife, water quality, and economics," says Collin. "The science of how humans fit into the ecosystem and how we affect it is constantly surprising. You can never lose your curiosity for nature in this job."

Respect for Trees

Trees have been helping Earth for hundreds of millions of years. We will never have as many trees and forests as we did 1,000 or even 100 years ago. But it's not too late to help protect the trees we have. It's never too late to plant new trees, either. Understanding how trees help Earth is an important first step. Planting, planning, and returning trees to their place in the ecosystem will help everyone on Earth for years to come.

DID YOU KNOW?
Wood is the only resource on Earth that is totally renewable, recyclable, reusable, *and* biodegradable.

PLANT A TREE

You can plant a tree, too! Spring and fall are the best times to plant trees. Here's how.

Step 1: Find out what kinds of trees will grow well in your area.

Step 2: Get a tree. Young trees for planting are available at tree nurseries. They usually come with their roots wrapped in a burlap ball.

Step 3: Dig a hole as deep as the ball and at least three times as wide.

Step 4: Carrying the tree by the root-ball, place the ball in the center of the hole. Remove the burlap. It's okay to leave the burlap in the hole. It will decompose.

Step 5: Fill the hole with the dirt you dug out of it as well as peat moss and composted manure (yes, manure!). This will give the tree a good foundation for getting the nutrients it needs.

Step 6: Water your tree daily. The tree will be thirsty. Give it about two or three gallons per watering. Do this for a month. After that, you can water it once a week. If it rains, then don't worry about watering the tree yourself.

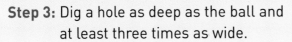

Name: Andrew Berry

Job: Forest Manager, Bernheim Arboretum & Research Forest, Clermont, Kentucky

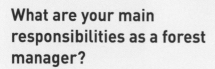

What are your main responsibilities as a forest manager?

Andrew Berry: As Forest Manager, I am responsible for overseeing the care, research, and inventory of our 14,000 acres of forest, grassland, and streams. We protect the full spectrum of plants and animals in Bernheim Forest, from the smallest insects to the largest mammals that roam our nation's lands.

How did you become interested in this type of work?

AB: I grew up in the country with fields and forest in my backyard. I spent most of my days outside, exploring our yard, which had no boundaries. I knew early on I wanted to be a wildlife biologist, and was encouraged by my parents to read and learn more about the natural world. The

more I learned, the more curious I became. I was not always a great student, but I was a good learner and never quit trying. After I graduated the University of Kentucky with a degree in natural resource conservation and management, I worked in the Rocky Mountains in Idaho and Yellowstone National Park. But I wanted to make a difference in my home state, so I returned to Kentucky. As an adult, I continue to learn and discover new facts about forests and wildlife through daily observations and reading.

What is a typical day at work for you?

AB: Bernheim Forest is a bustling place, with something new and unexpected nearly every day. A typical day might include searching for rare plants and animals, leading an educational hike, meeting with researchers, or improving habitats in the forest. Sometimes work can be strenuous and days are long; other times it is so beautiful at Bernheim that you forget it is a job.

What are some challenges and rewards you have had in your work?

AB: It is a delicate balance between connecting people with nature and the need to protect nature from people. I work to help people see wildlife, but I also have to remember that wildlife do not always want to see people. My greatest successes come from the sum of smaller accomplishments, such as the thousands of smiles on students' faces and the hundreds of turtles and snakes that I help cross the road every year.

What do you enjoy most about your work?

AB: I most enjoy knowing that I play a role in protecting Bernheim Forest's clean water, inspiring forests, diverse plant communities, and healthy wildlife populations so that future generations can enjoy them as much as we do now.

What is the most important thing kids should know about forests?

AB: A forest is much more than a bunch of plants. While trees are the largest and most visible features, many other species of plants and animals, as well as the soils, rocks, and water contribute to the richness of a forest and the ecosystem. In addition to their importance within the ecosystem, forests contribute to the richness of the local community in the educational, cultural, and recreational opportunities they offer visitors.

Check it out: bernheim.org

Glossary

bark	the tough outer covering of a tree
blight	a plant disease
carbon dioxide	a gas that plants need to grow
cellulose	tiny fibers that hold together the wood of a tree
deforestation	the removal or clearing an area of forests or trees
drought	a long period of dry weather
ecosystem	a system made up of living things interacting with their environment
endangered	threatened with total loss
forestry	the science and practice of caring for forests
habitat	the natural home or environment of an animal, plant, or other organism
sap	the fluid part of a tree
species	a class of living things of the same kind and with the same name
sustainable	able to keep going

FOR MORE INFORMATION

Books

Jakubiak, David J. *What Can We do About Deforestation?* Rosen Publishing, 2011.

Mason, Paul. *Forests Under Threat*. Heinemann Library, 2010.

Web Sites

Discover the Forest: *Find a forest to explore near you.* www.discovertheforest.org

Real Trees 4 Kids: *Learn all about trees and tree farming.* http://www.realtrees4kids.org/threefive.htm

Rainforest Allliance Kids' Corner: *Learn important facts about the world's rainforests.* www.rainforest-alliance.org/kids

All web addresses (URLs) have been reviewed carefully by our editors. Web sites change, however, and we cannot guarantee that a site's future contents will continue to meet our high standards of quality and educational value.

Index

About the Author

Anne Flounders has lots of on-the-job experience writing for kids and teens. She has written and edited magazines, nonfiction books, teachers' guides, reader's theater plays, and web content. She has also recorded narration for audio- and ebooks. Anne protects our green Earth with her husband and son in Connecticut.